Doctor Swears

Vulgar Word Coloring Book
To Rant & Relax

By

S.B. Nozaz

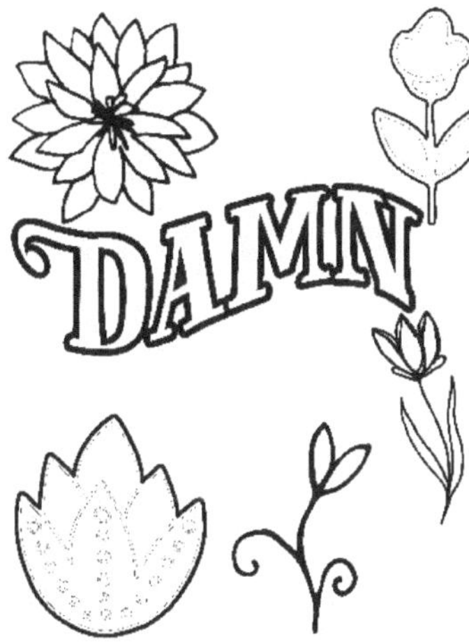

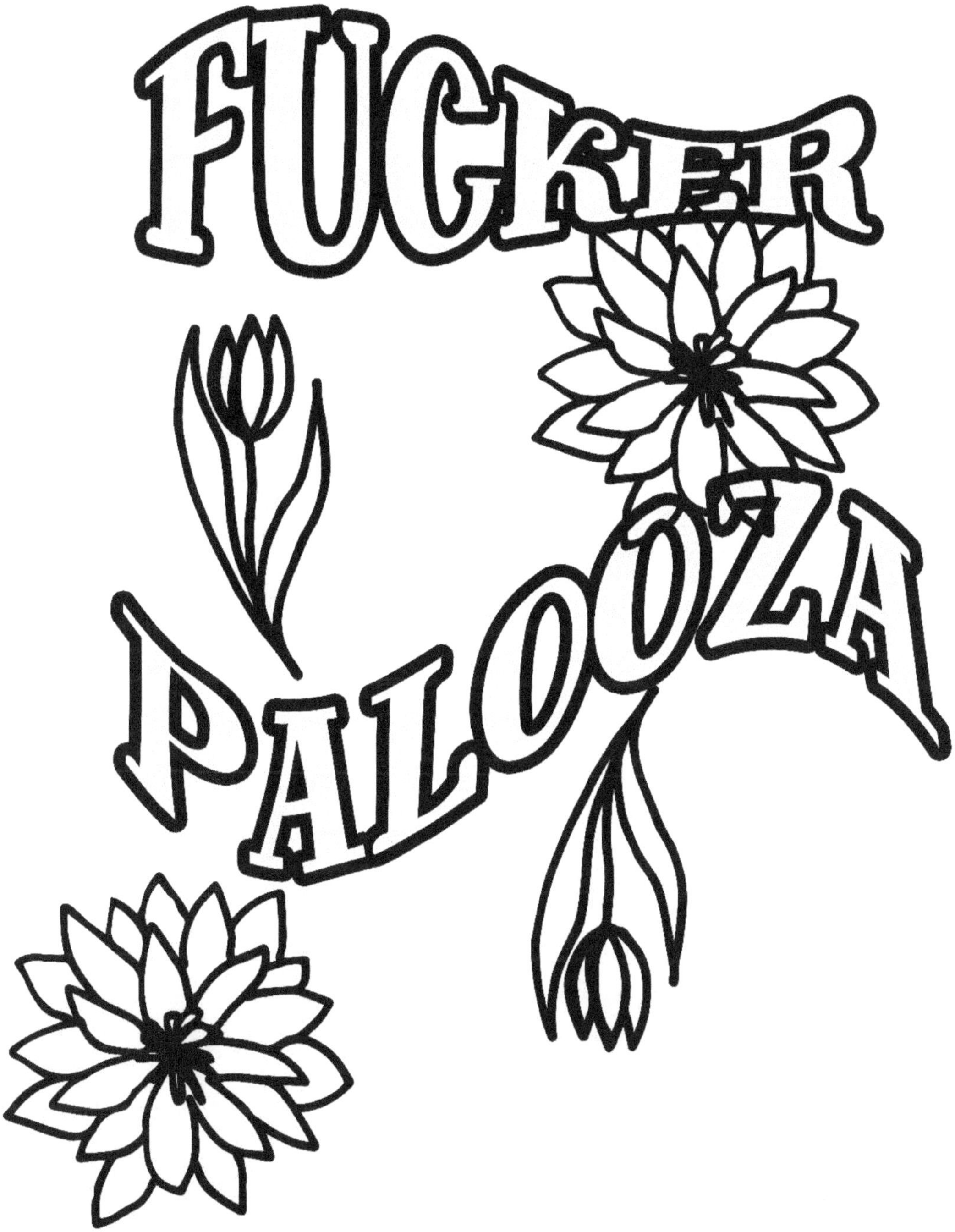
FUCKER
PALOOZA

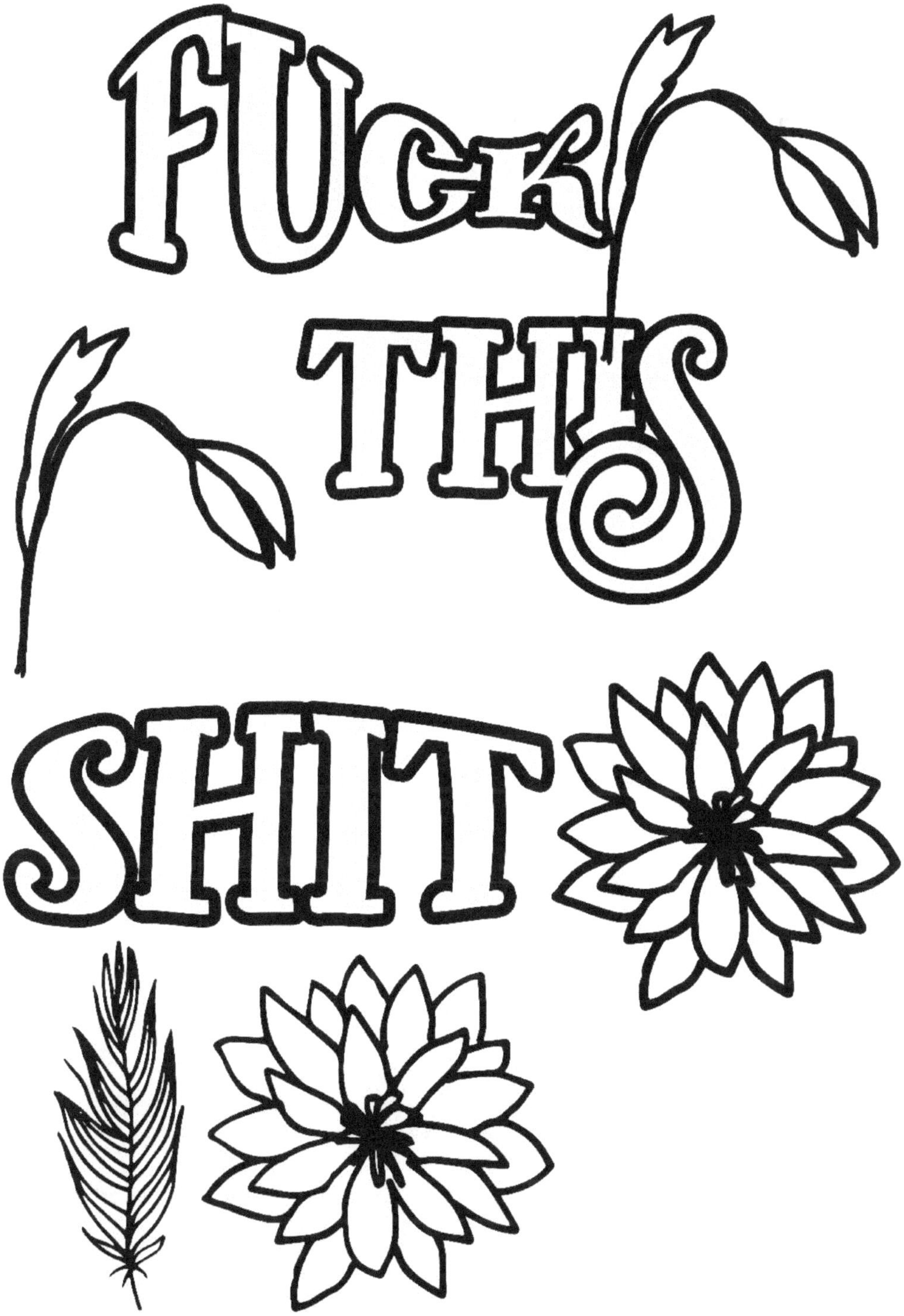
FUCK THIS SHIT

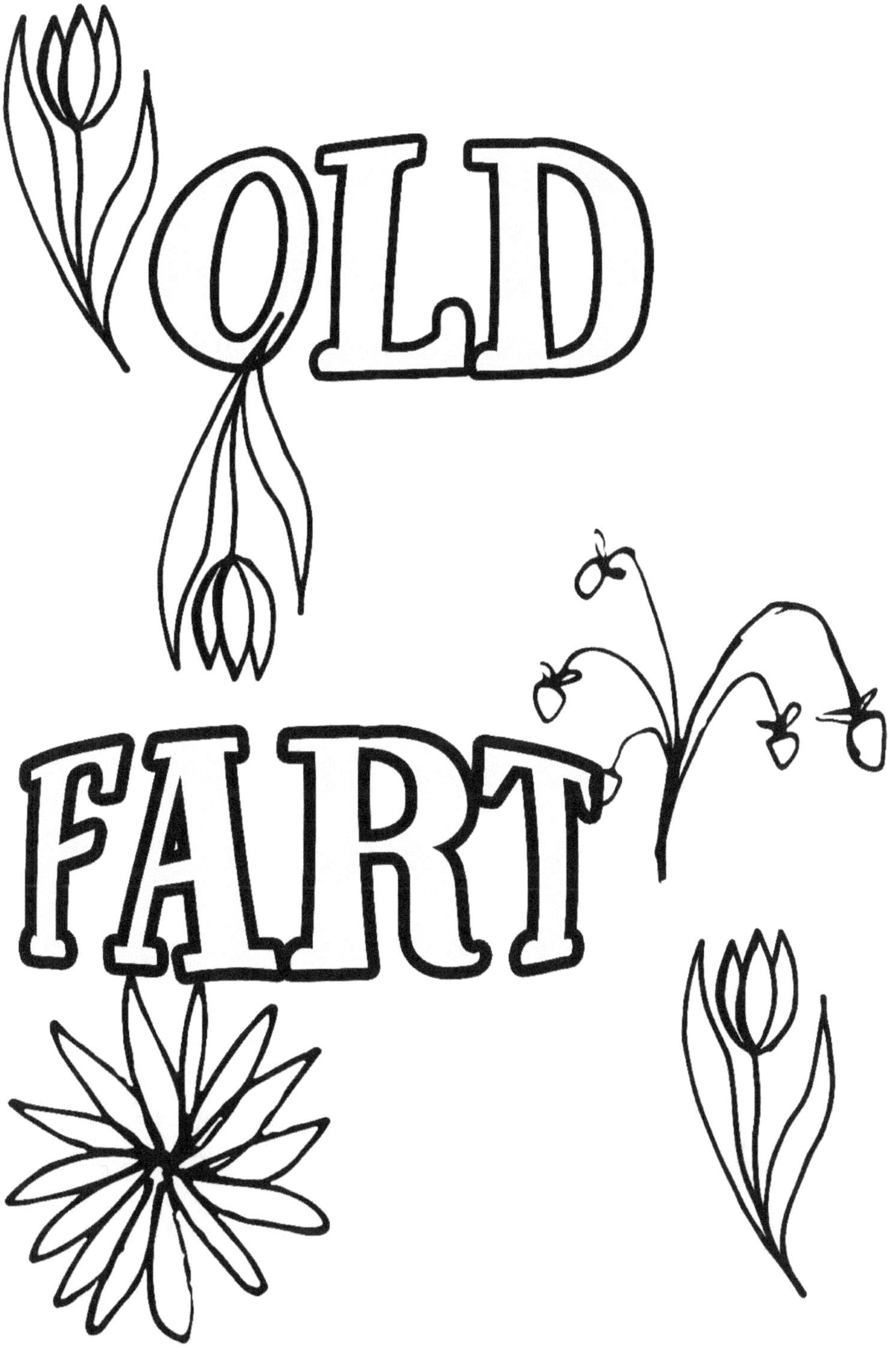
OLD
FART

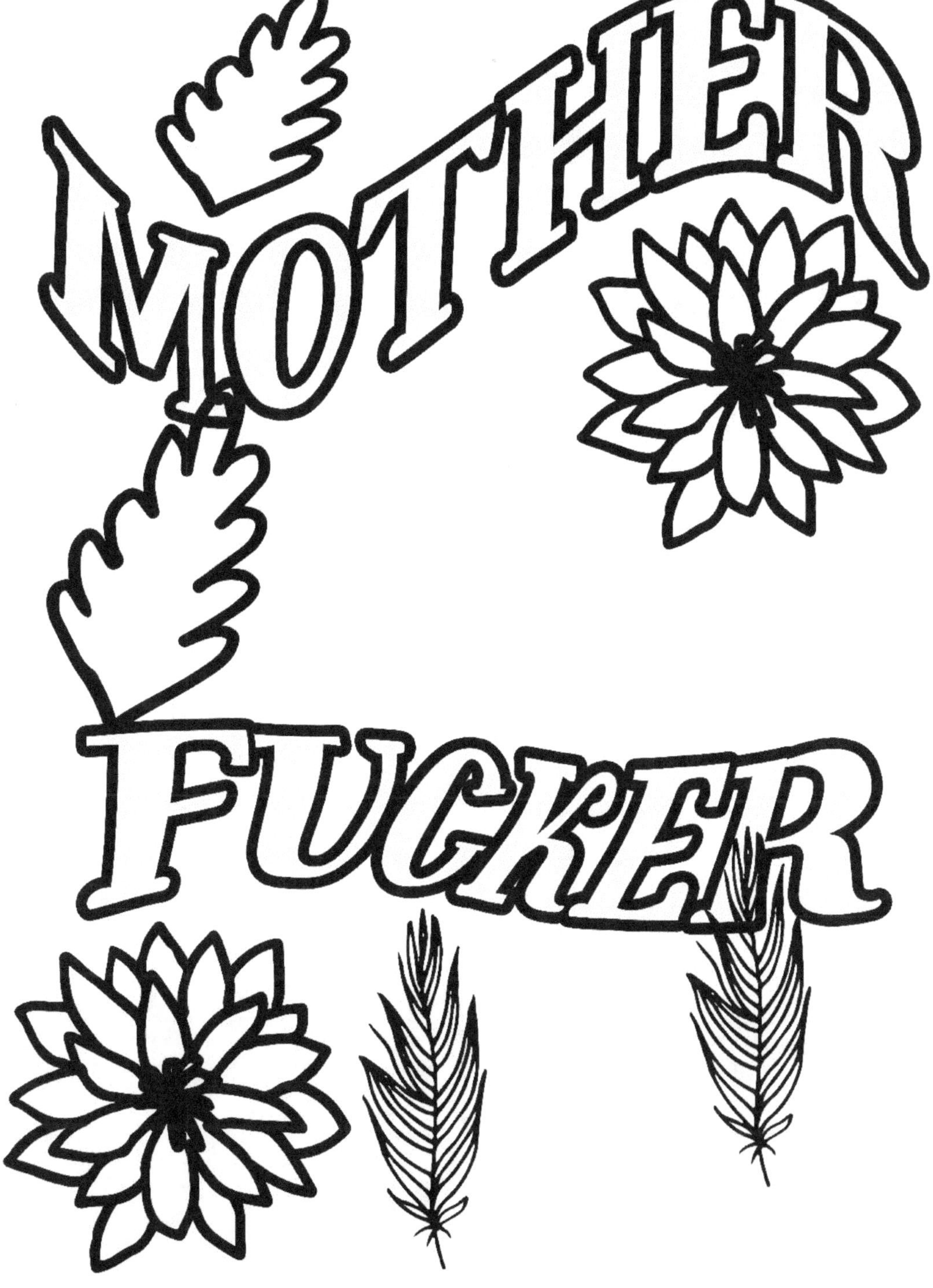
MOTHER
FUCKER

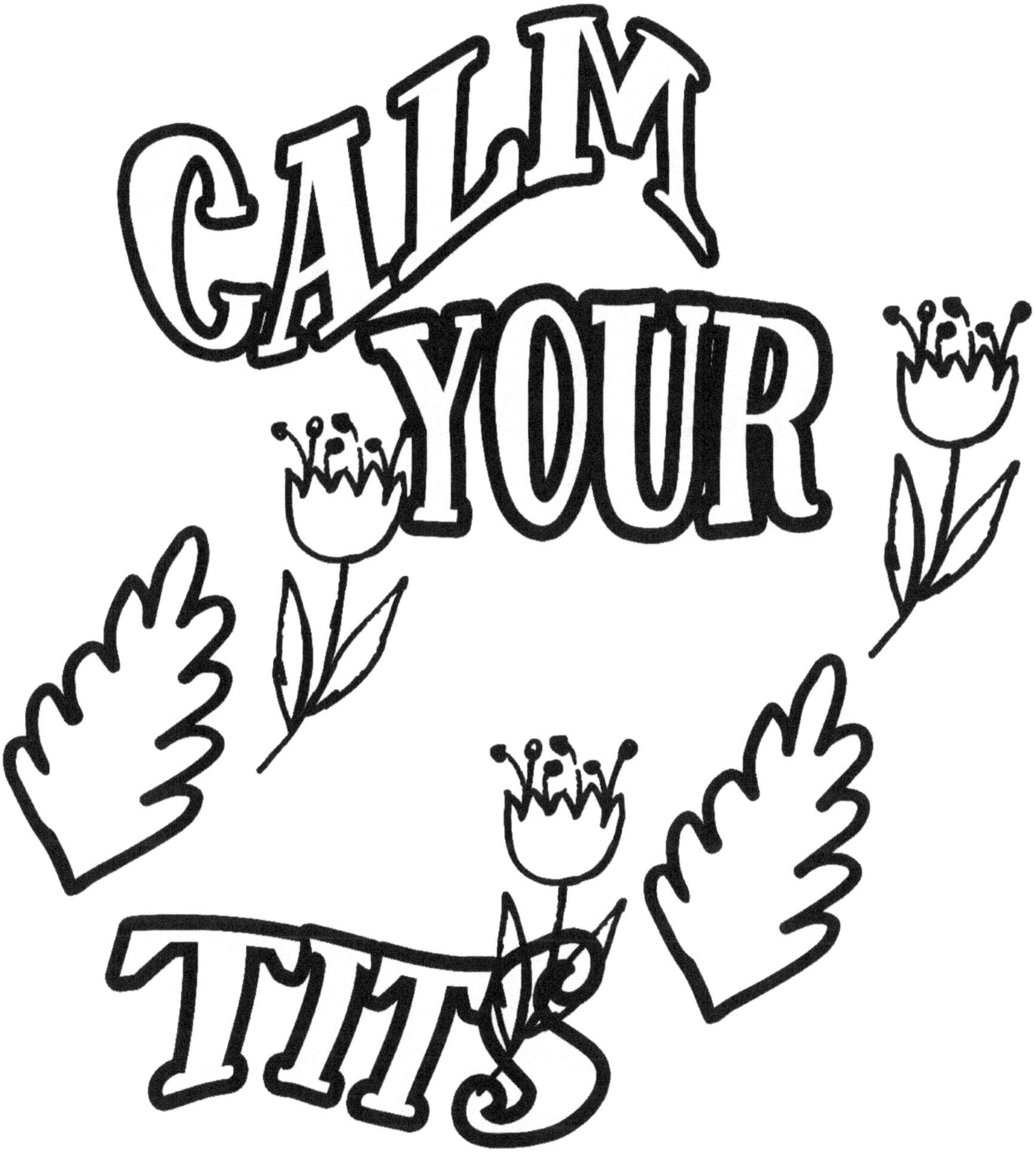
CALM
YOUR
TITS

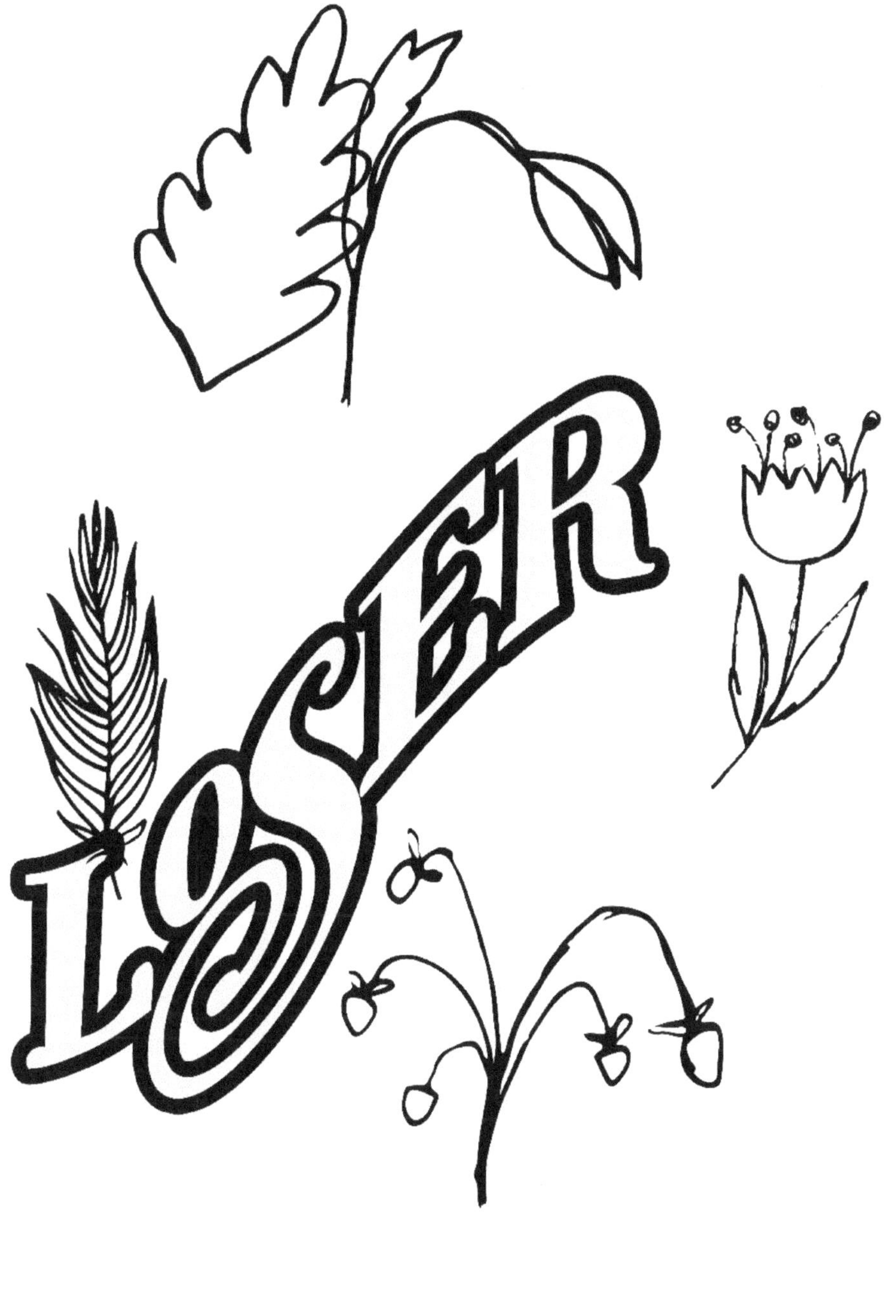
LOSER

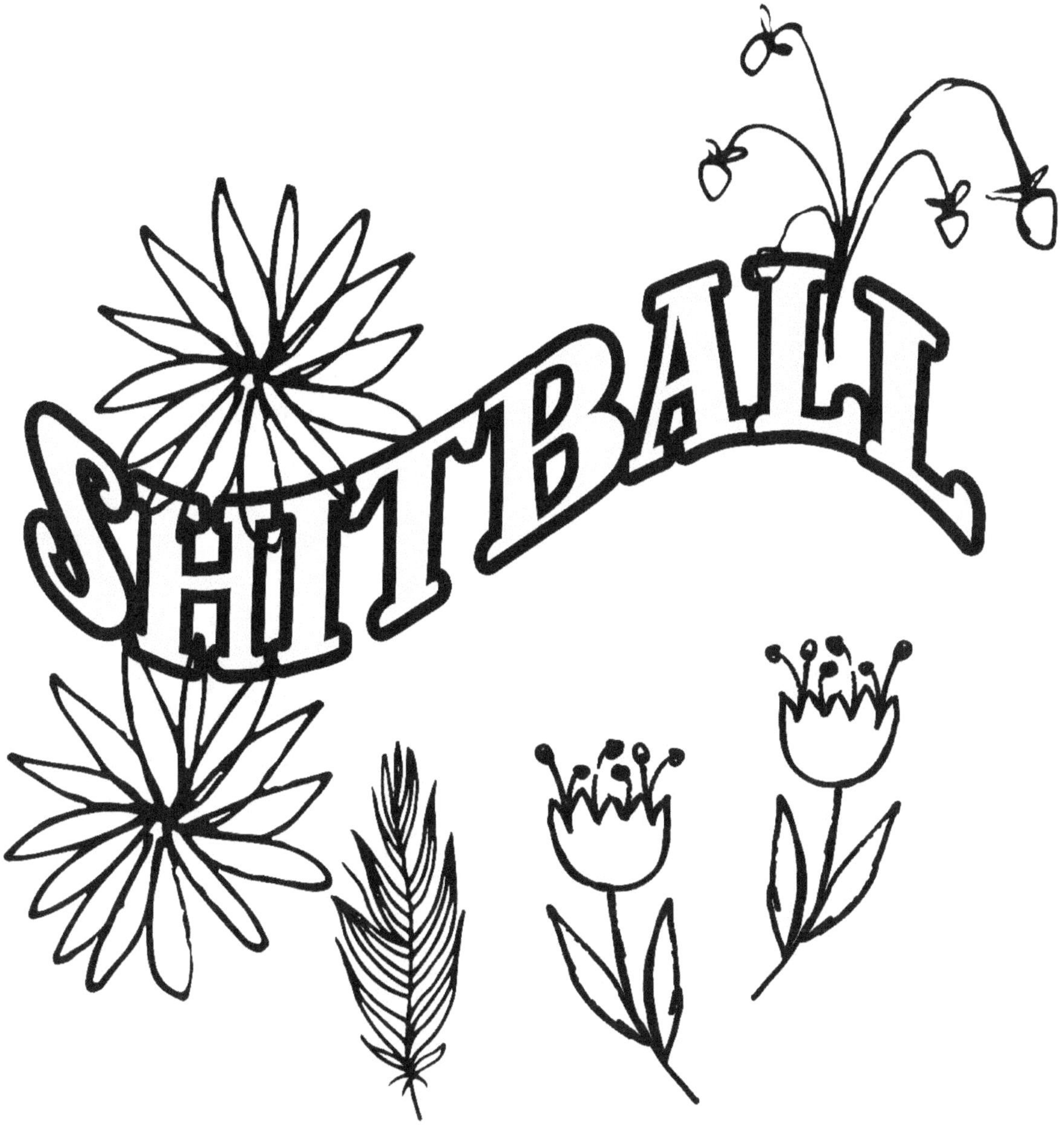
SHITBALL

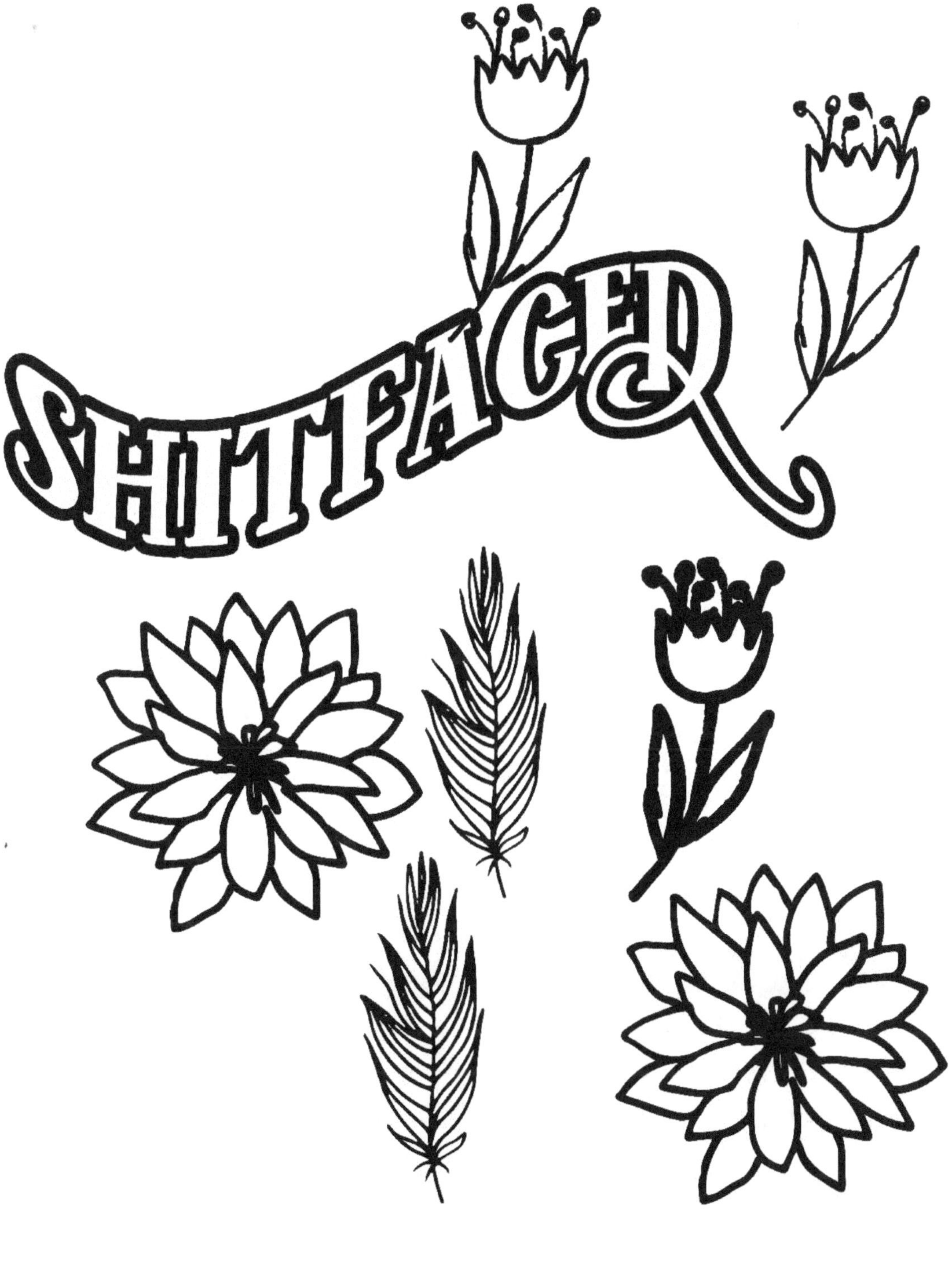
SHITFACED

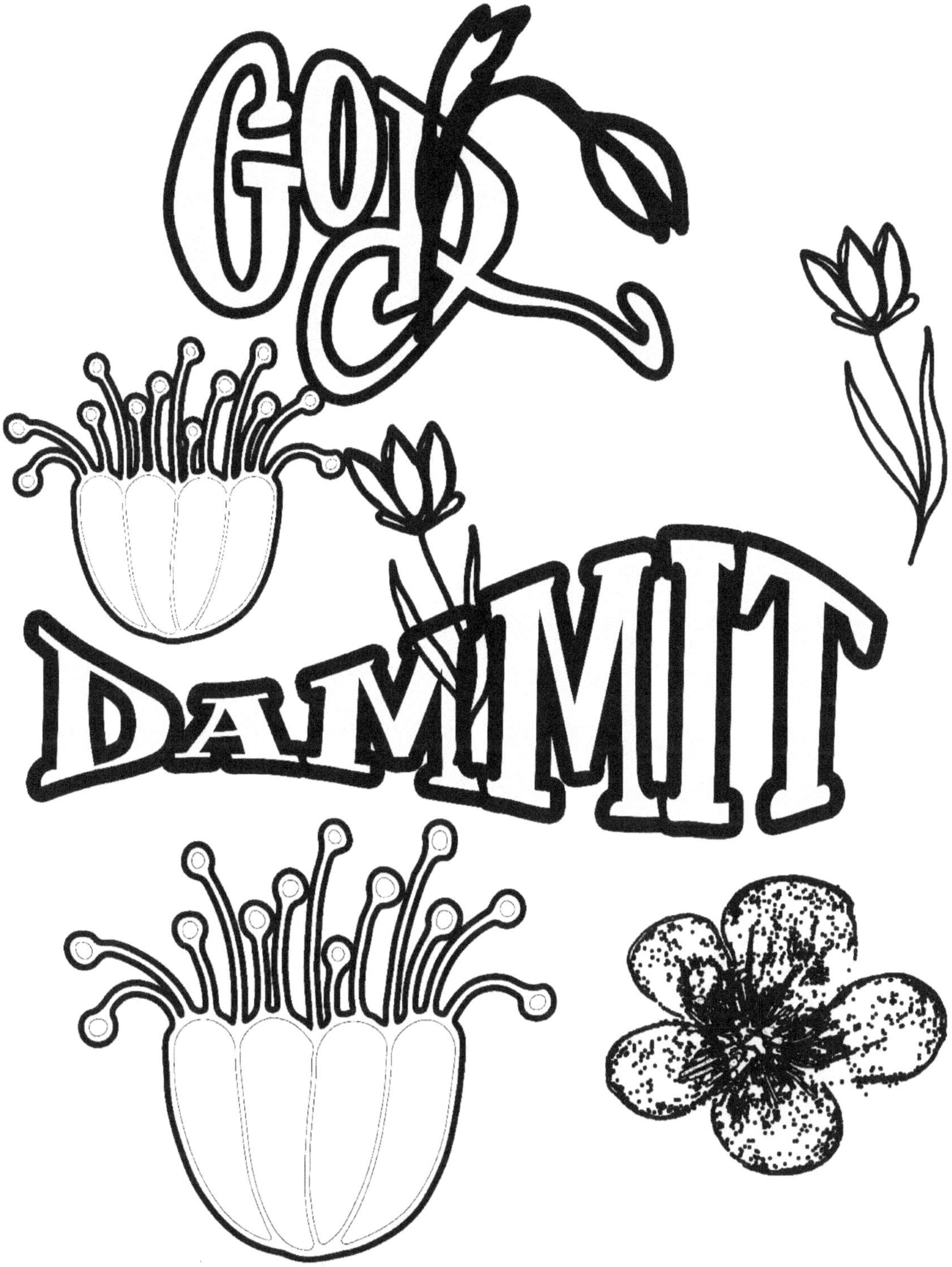
GOD
DAMMIT

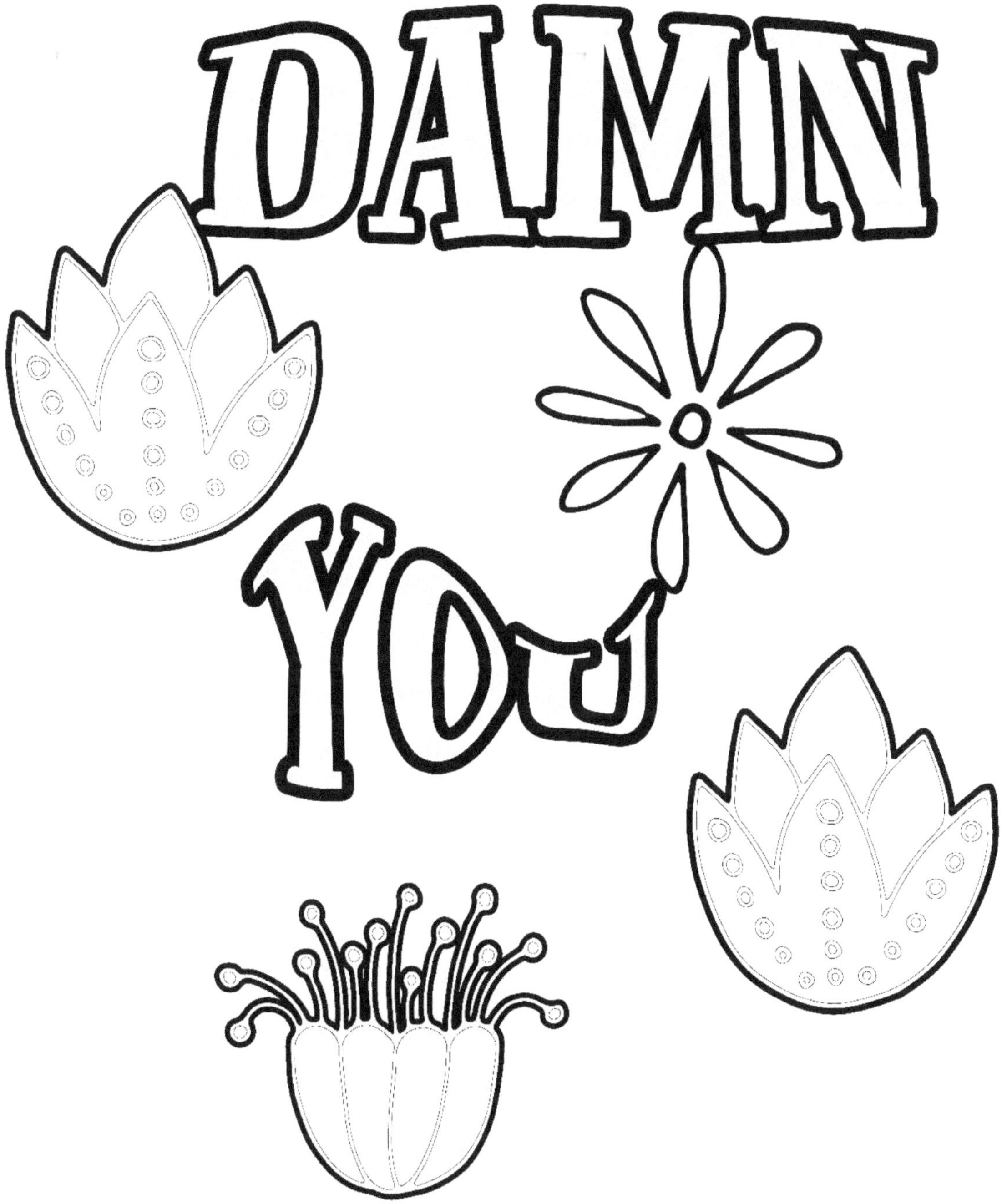
DAMN
YOU

GO TO
HELL

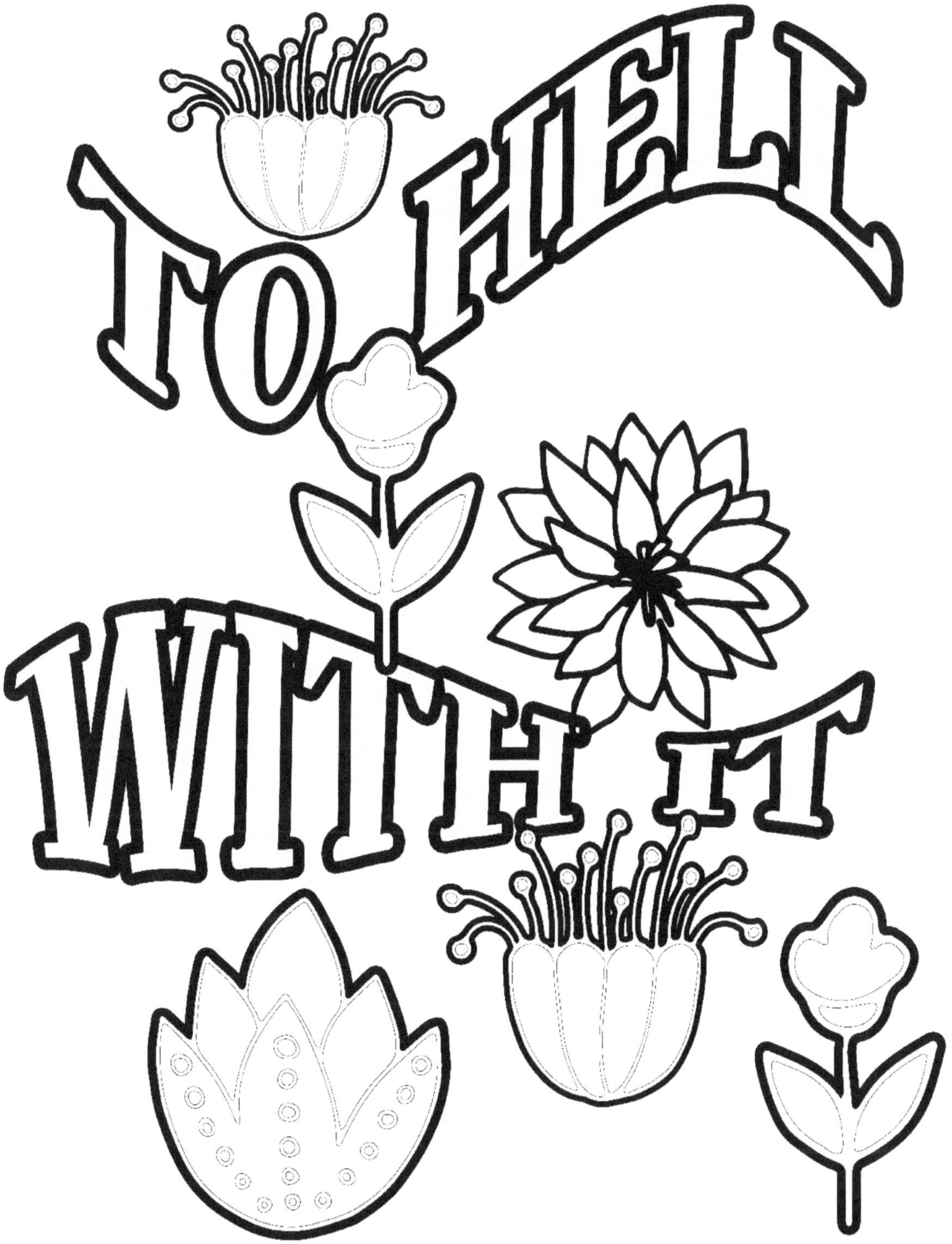
TO HELL
WITH IT

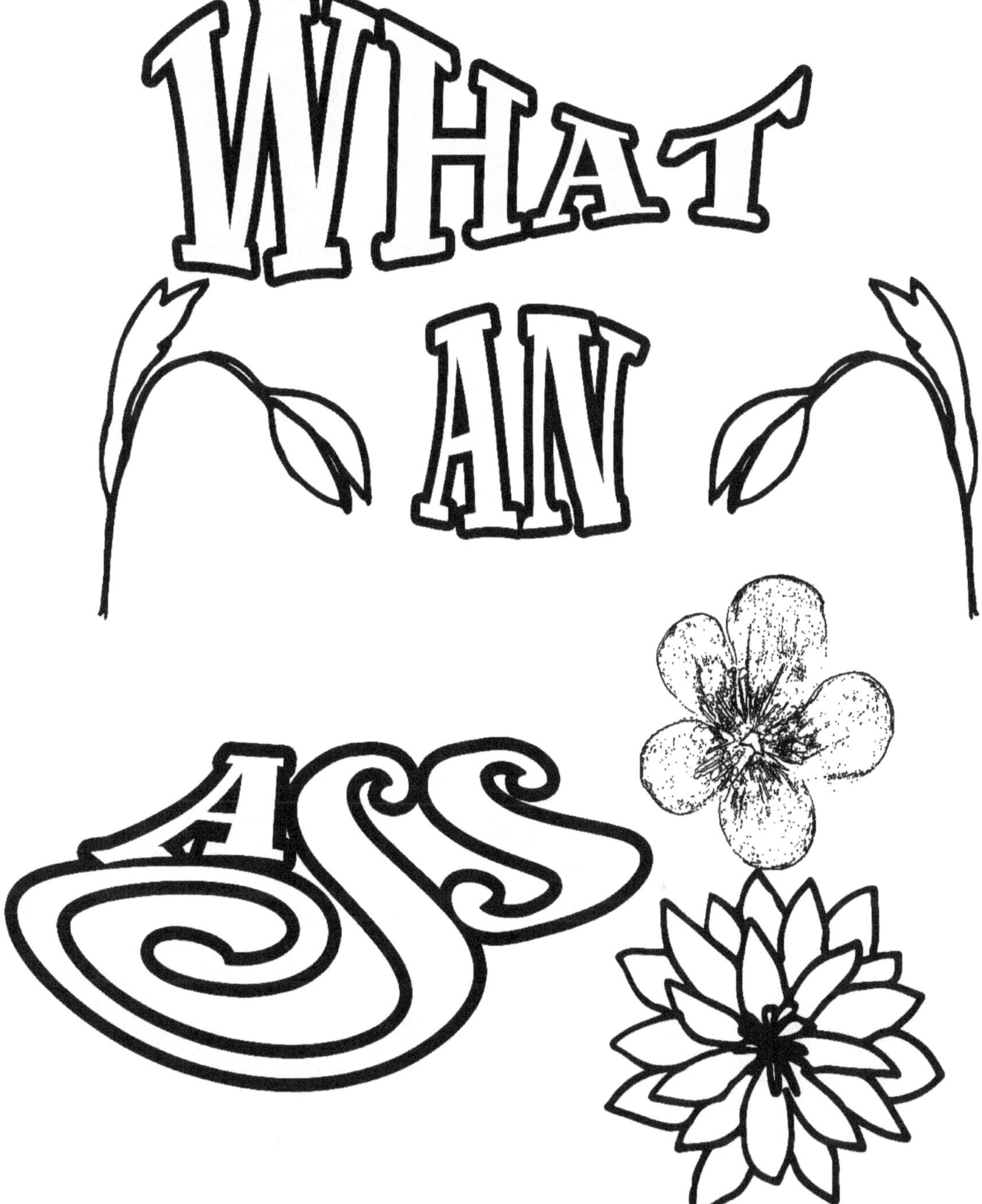
WHAT
AN
ASS

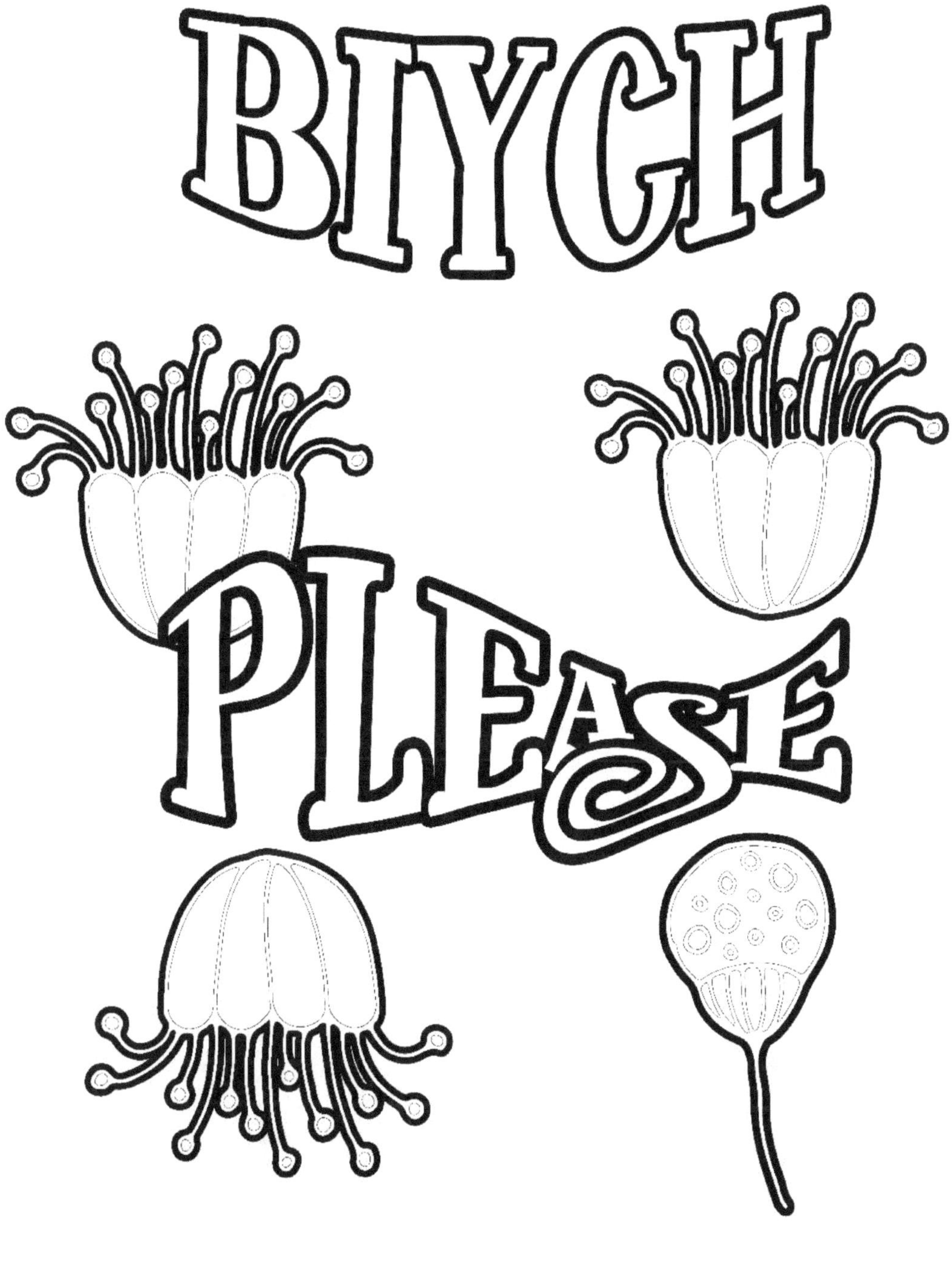
BIYCH
PLEASE

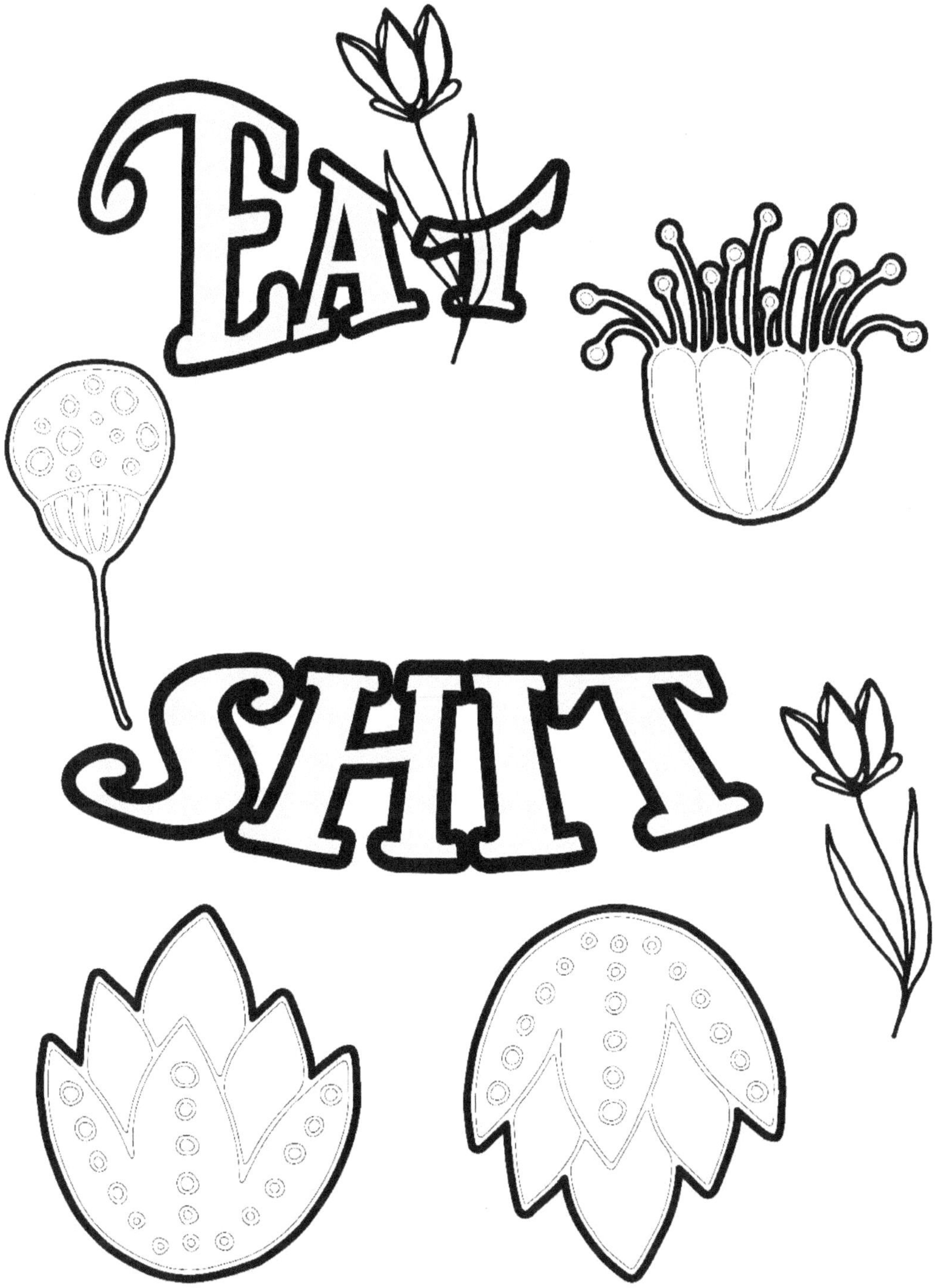
EAT
SHIT

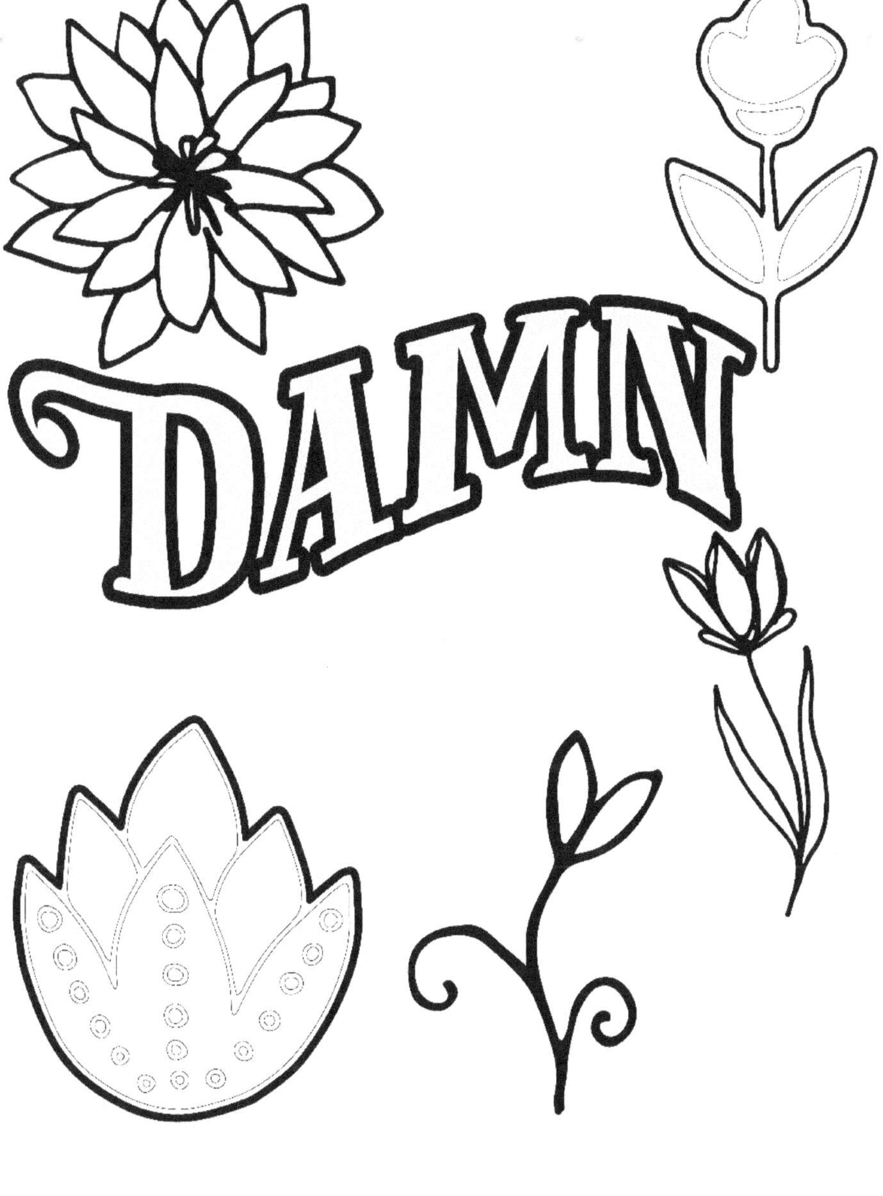
DAMN

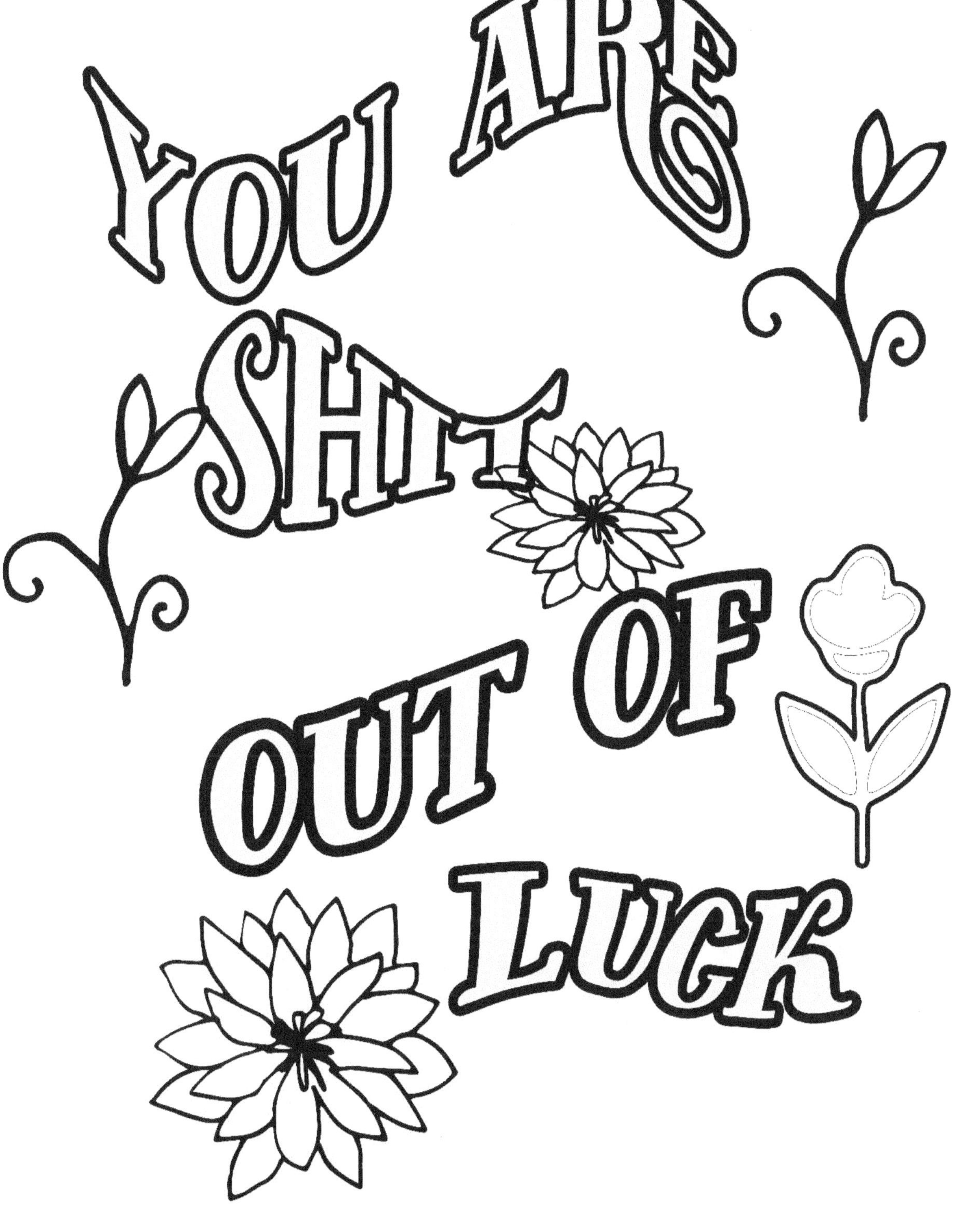
YOU ARE
SHIT
OUT OF
LUCK

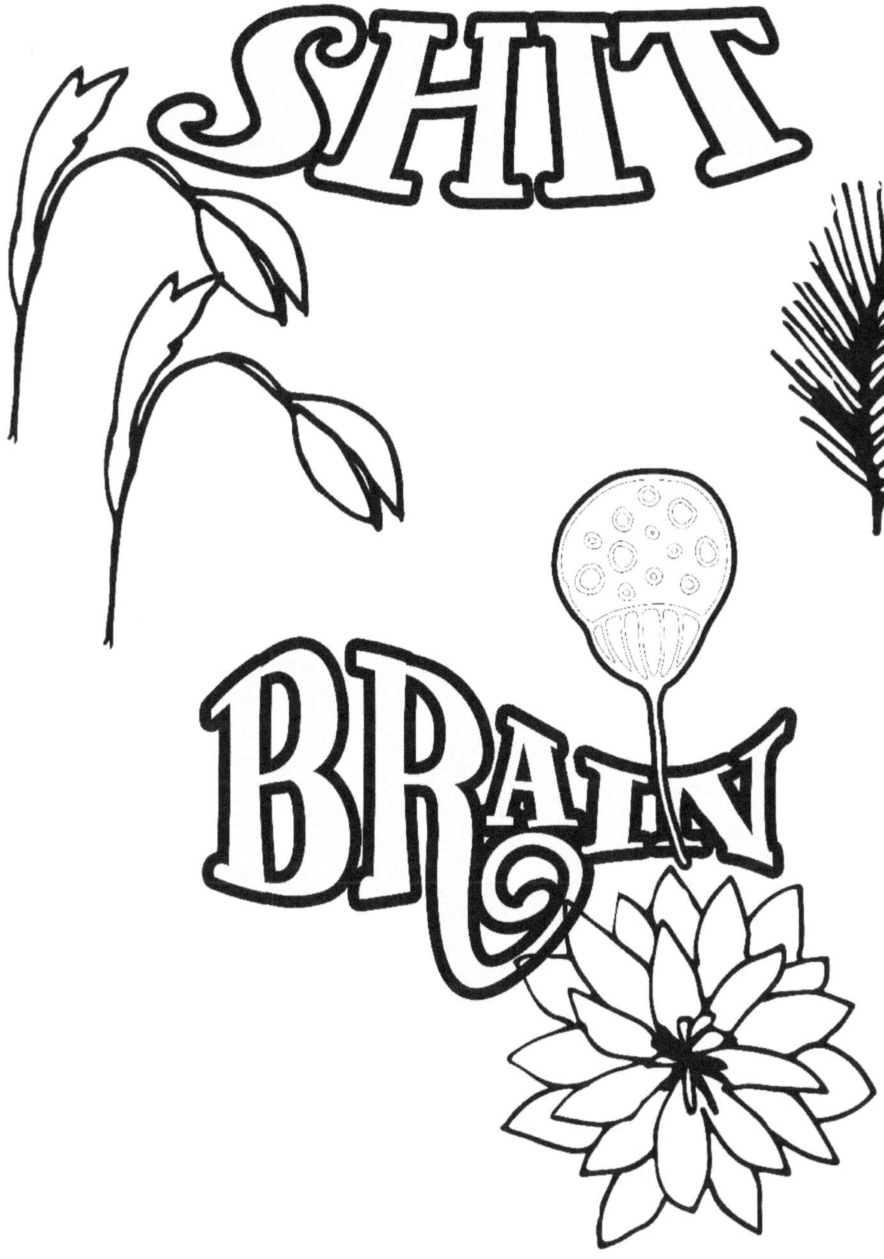
SHIT
BRAIN

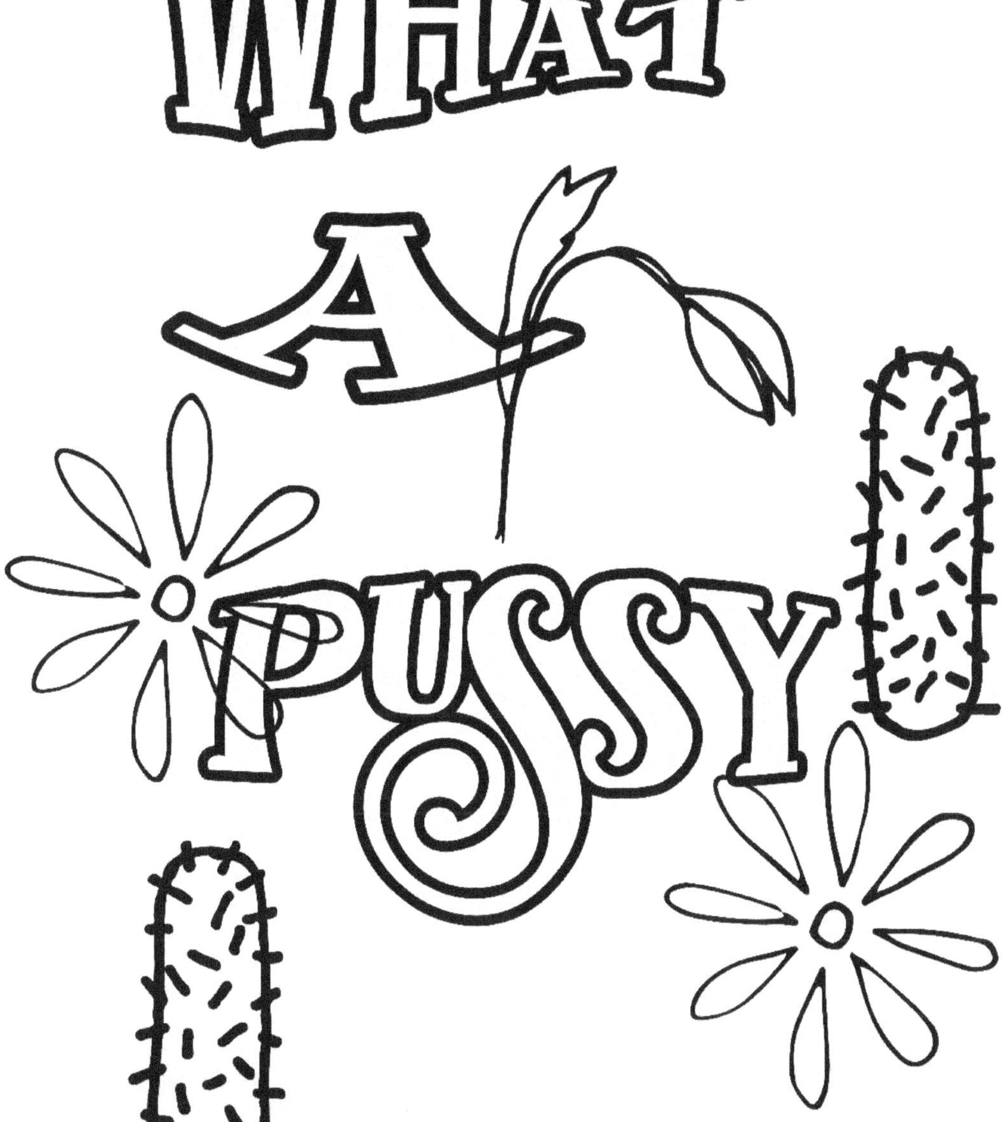
WHAT
A
PUSSY

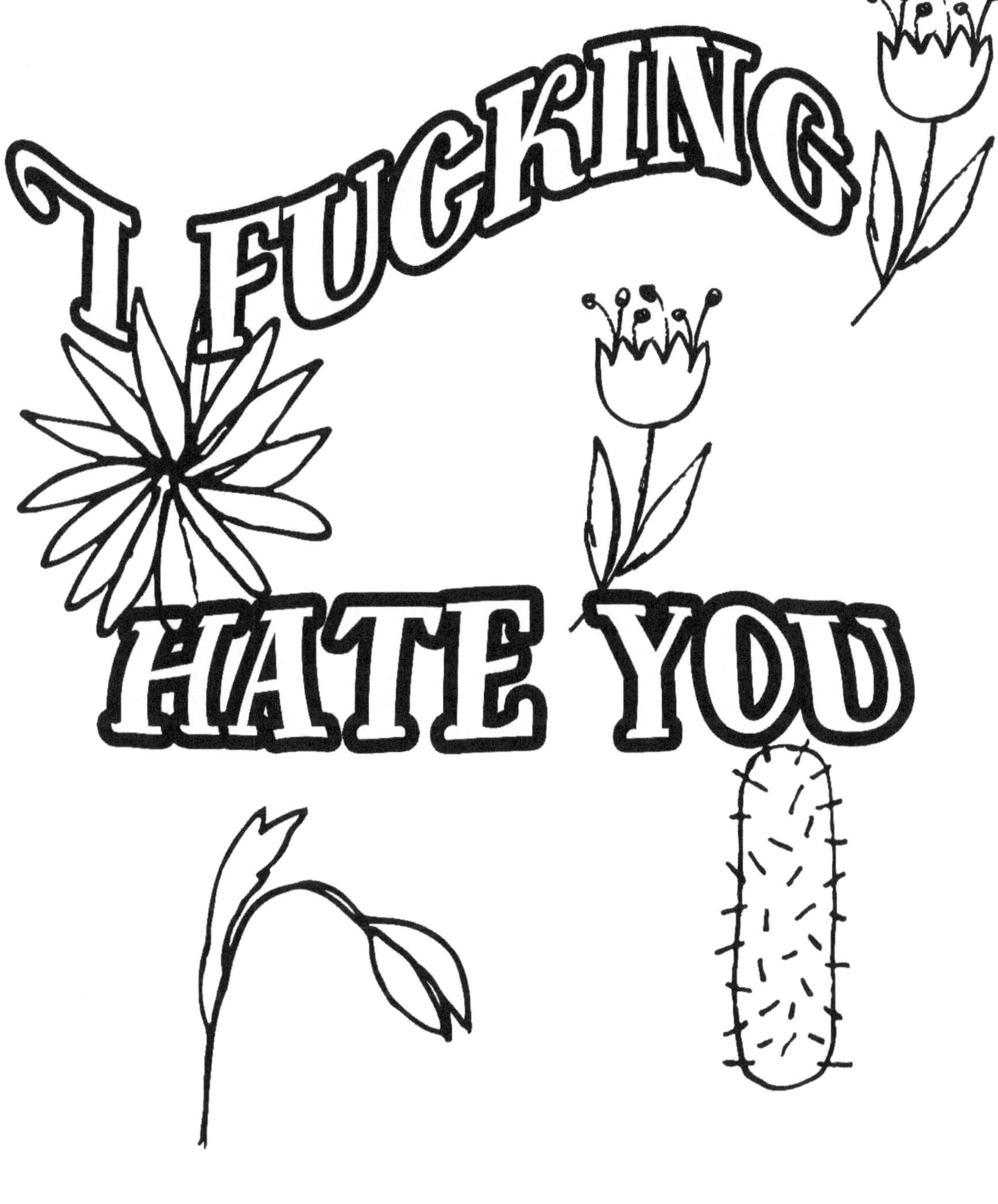
I FUCKING
HATE YOU

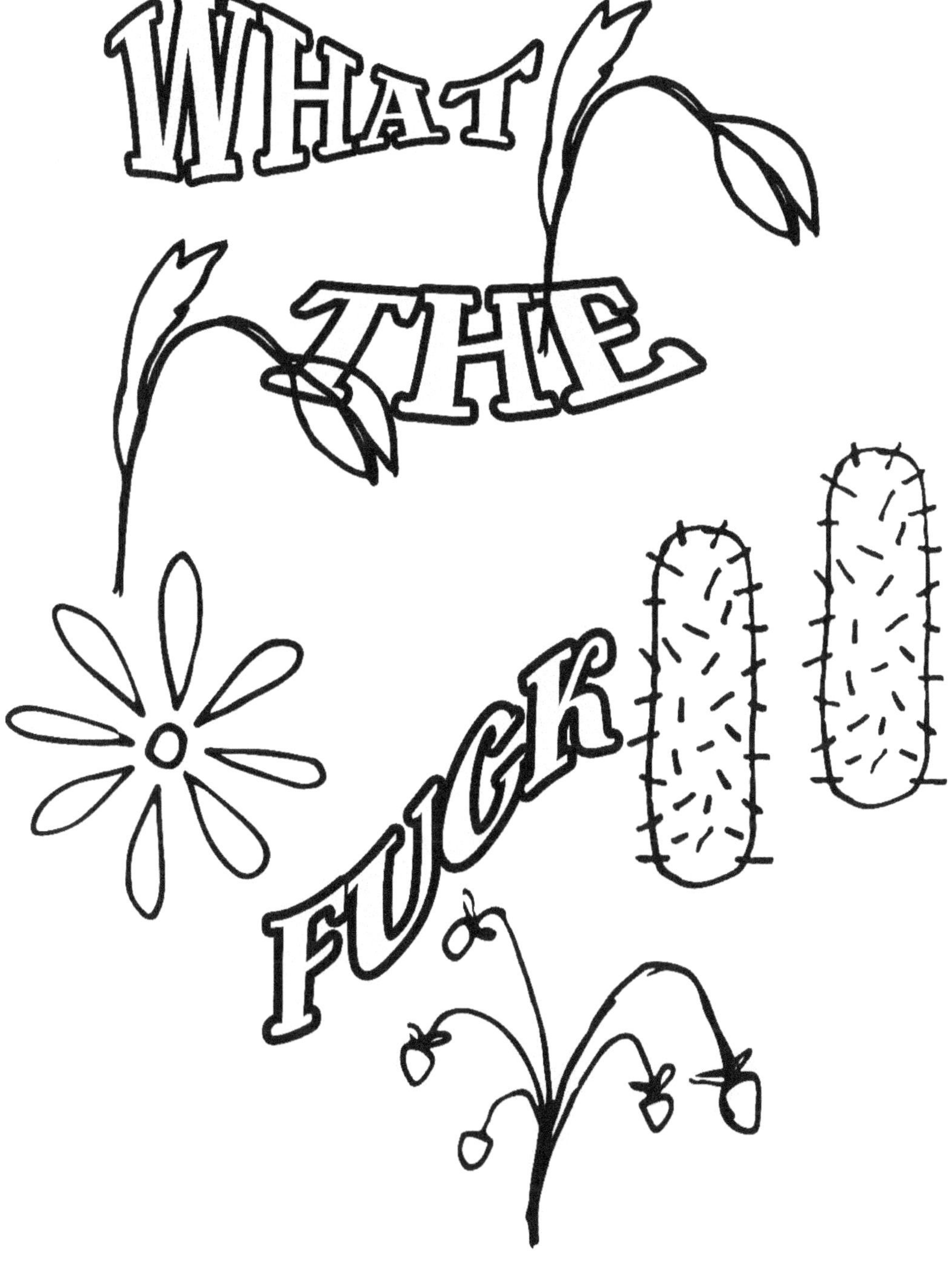
WHAT
THE
FUCK

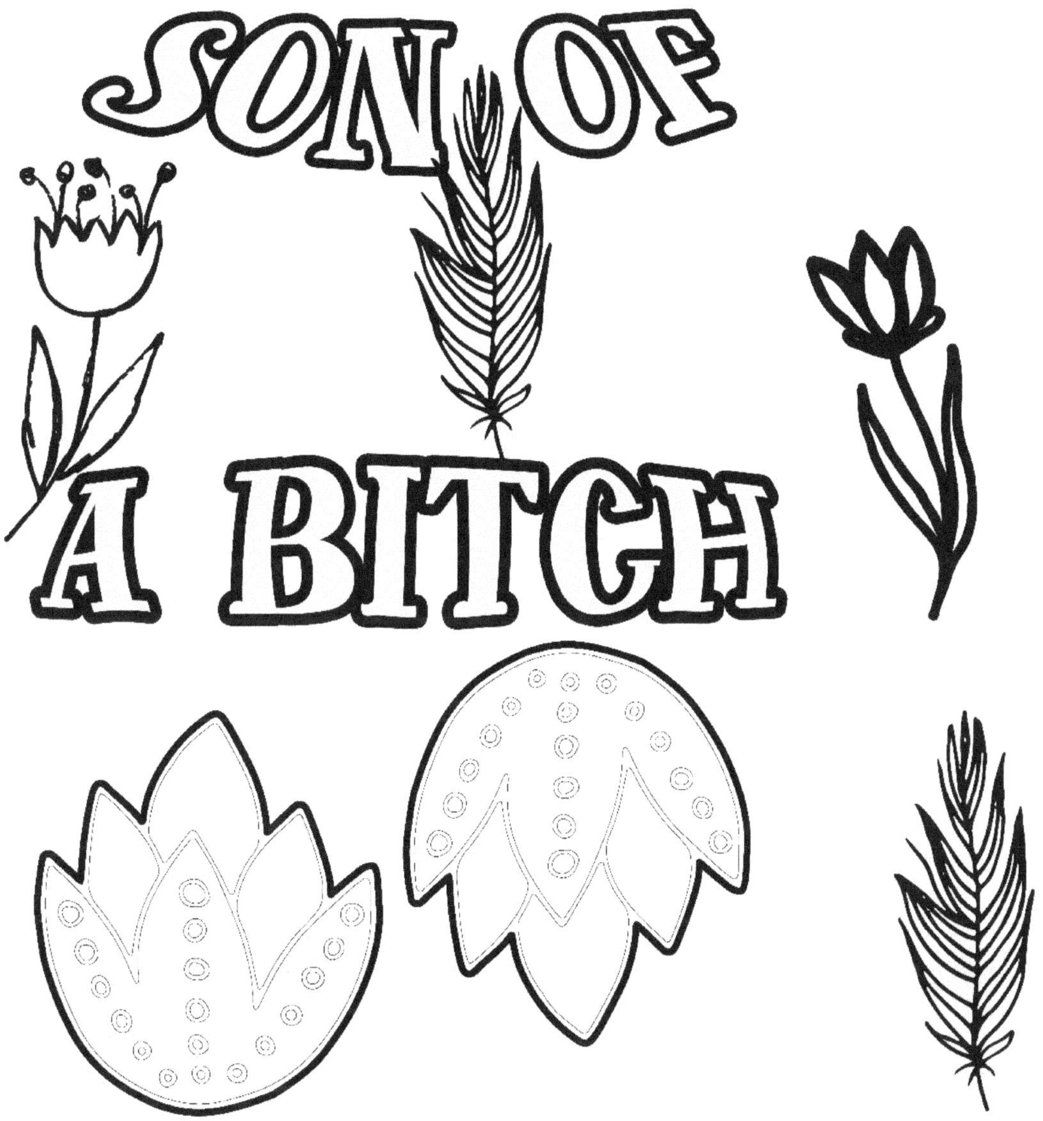
SON OF
A BITCH

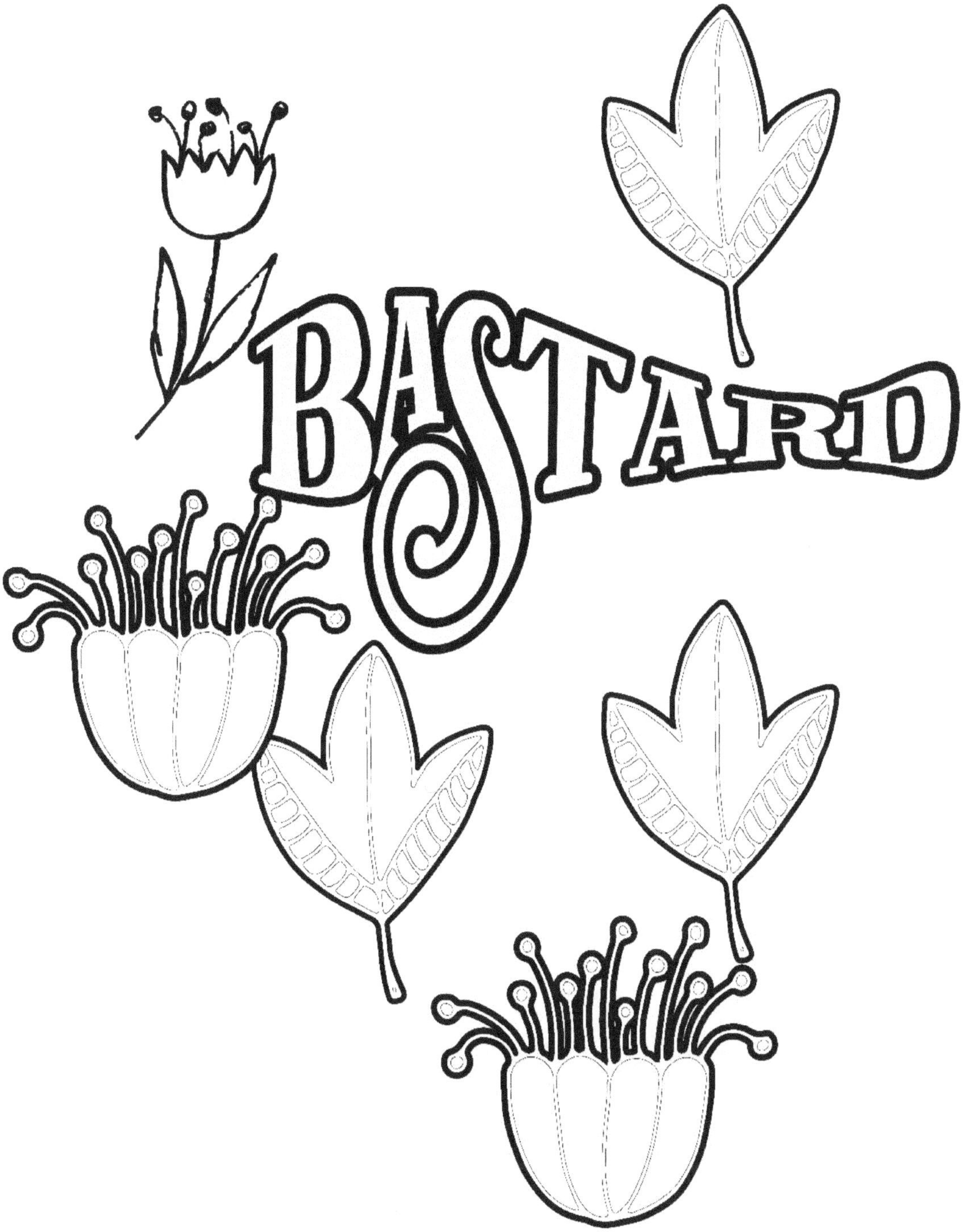
BASTARD

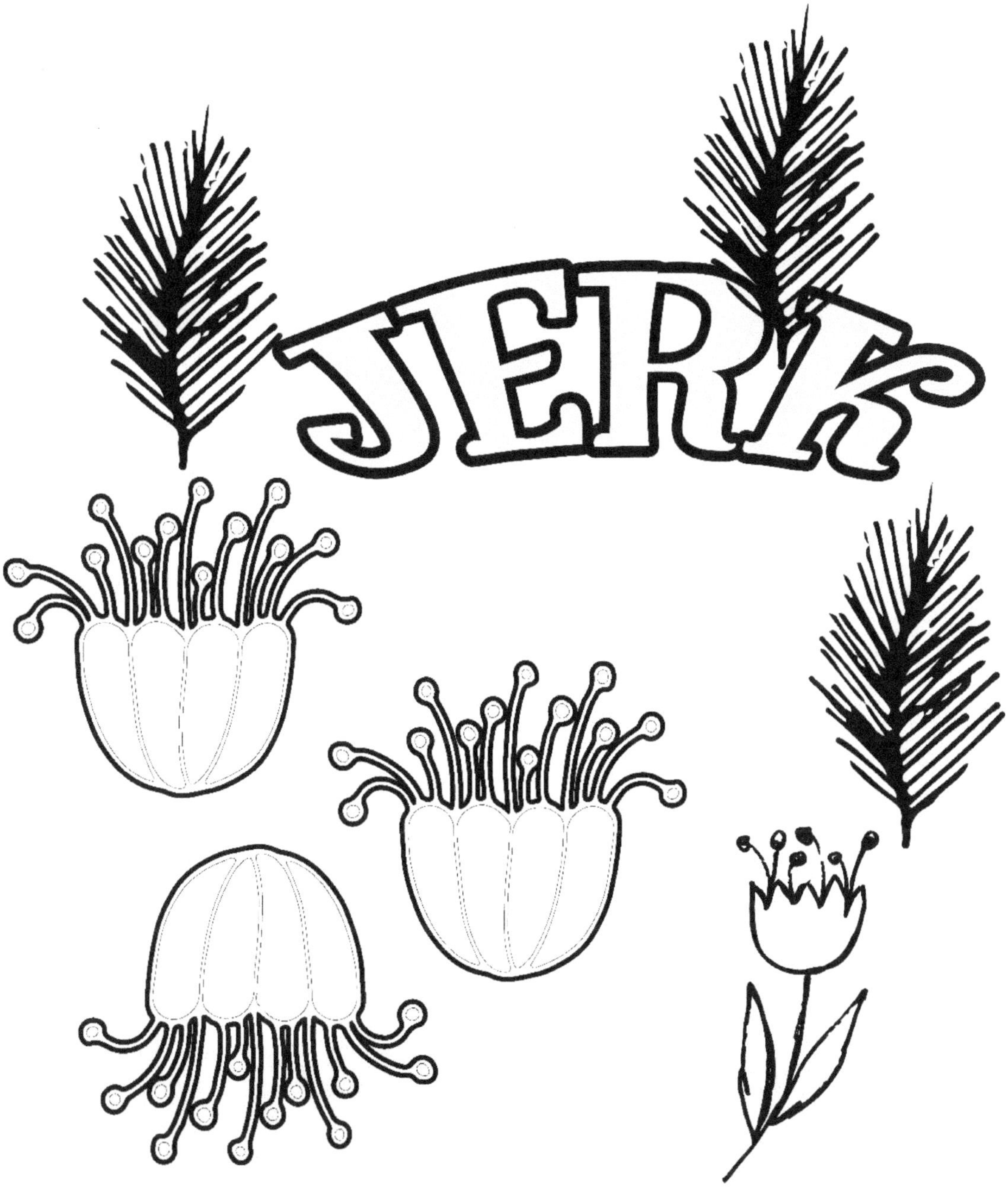
JERK

Note

www.ingramcontent.com/pod-product-compliance
Lightning Source LLC
Chambersburg PA
CBHW080638190526
45169CB00009B/3422